LETTERS FOR ALL SEASONS

LETTERS FOR ALL SEASONS

Herbert Mather

 Abingdon Press

Letters for All Seasons: Telling the Church's Story by Mail

93 94 95 96 97 98 99 00 01 02 — 10 9 8 7 6 5 4 3 2 1

This book is printed on acid-free recycled paper.

Library of Congress Cataloging-in-Publication Data

Mather, Herbert.
    Letters for all seasons / Herbert Mather.
       p.   cm.
    Includes bibliographical references.
    ISBN 0-687-39343-4 (pbk. : alk. paper)
    1. Stewardship, Christian.   2. Church finance.   3. Letter-writing.
I. Title.
BV772.M384   1993
254.4—dc20   93-12892
                                                    CIP

CONTENTS

TELLING THE CHURCH'S STORY
BY MAIL

Every congregation, regardless of its size, needs better communication systems. Never assume that "all our members know what is going on." They don't.

Twenty persons from a church of about 225 members sat in a circle. They were attending a Council on Ministries planning retreat. Each one described one program or activity in the church that he or she found meaningful. About two-thirds of the way around a circle a woman said, "I really appreciate the prayer chain. I receive calls day and night. It makes me feel good to be called upon to pray specifically for needs of persons in our church and in our community." The person sitting next to her exclaimed, "I didn't know we had a prayer chain in this church."

The church has a story to tell. We want the story to be heard. The search for tools that convey the message and excite the hearer is a never-ending task. Letters can't do the whole job, but they can be an effective part of the total task of communication. A letter is a means of communication. Churches are in the communication business.

Letters are an effective and helpful tool to communicate the mission and ministry of the church. They are more personal than articles in a church newsletter. Good letters are usually short, forcing us to choose our words carefully. They communicate feelings as well as facts, both of which are important.

Two Programs

This manual contains two programs. The resource will assist any church that is serious about communicating with its members and constituents. The first program is a 12-month letter-writing plan.

The guide suggests a strategy to get the program approved by the appropriate governing body of the congregation. In most churches, the Finance Committee is the logical group to steer the process even though these are not, strictly speaking, fund-raising letters.

In the first section (pages 9-38) you will find the LETTERS FOR ALL SEASONS twelve-month letter plan. Complete instructions describe monthly topics, suggestions for letter writers, and timelines. Sample letters for each month are included. They focus on our relationship with God, God's creatures, and the creation. They are about the mission and ministry of the church. They are about commitment.

The goal of *Letters for All Seasons* is to:

a) tell the story of the church's ministry throughout the world, especially the mission and ministry of your congregation within your community.

b) encourage participation in the mission of the church through inspiration and information.

c) provide motivation for persons to give their time and material resources through the ministry of their congregation.

In business terms, most churches will find it cost effective to send monthly letters to the congregation's members and constituents. This manual provides a complete description of how to do the best job possible in your church with a series of *Letters for All Seasons*.

Section II (beginning on page 39) is a letter-writing financial campaign plan. It is a guide to a letter-writing financial commitment campaign. We could call this part "Letters for a Brief Season." You will find detailed instructions and model letters.

Letters are not meant to be the only source of communication with the people, but they are a good means of telling the story. This manual is designed to help you use letters more effectively in your total communications program.

—Herb Mather

SECTION ONE

LETTERS FOR ALL SEASONS

CHAPTER I - WHAT GOOD IS A LETTER?

Most churches send letters to members. In fact, most churches send letters each year to members about money. For the greatest number of churches, the question is not whether we will send letters but:

a) How many will we send?
b) When will we send them?
c) What will they say?

Letters have a long and important history for Christians. Most of the New Testament was written as letters. Historians study the letters of Martin Luther, John Calvin, John Wesley, and other Christian leaders through the centuries, to understand their life and times.

People like to get letters. They report stories. They ask questions. They express emotions. They signify relationships. They help the writer as well as the reader.

Members and friends of your church like to hear about exciting things that are happening. They want to know about people. They want to know what difference the church is making in their community and around the world. They like to rejoice with those who rejoice. Don't even deny them the right to weep with those who weep.

A recent Gallup study of volunteering and giving in America discovered that letters were a very effective means to get persons *started* on giving. Nineteen percent of respondents reported that they contributed to an organization for the first time in the past year. The most frequently cited reason for doing so was "that they received a letter asking them to give (30 percent)" (page 4, *Giving and Volunteering in the United States*, The Independent Sector, Washington, D.C., 1990).

Letters help make connections. A giver cannot go everywhere the giver's money goes. The church dispenses the funds through many ministries at home and abroad. Letters can tell stories that help persons link (connect) with the people who are ministered to by the money.

Generous gifts do not give the donor a right to tell the church how it should spend the money. Christian givers are not seeking power or control. Generous givers appreciate the opportunity to hear stories of what their gifts have done and will do in the name of Jesus Christ.

A letter is also a reminder. It helps a person remember commitments. It invites the examination of priorities. Each letter broadens the reader's world by introducing another experience or story from the perspective of the writer.

Letters can go to everyone. Announcements in worship services are heard only by those in the pews. Inserts in worship bulletins are read by few of the worship attenders. Only those persons who attend worship will hear an announcement, and only half of those who attend will read an insert. A letter can arrive in the homes of everyone—even those who do not attend. It is more likely to be read than a bulletin insert.

A recent study by Dr. Edward Uthe of the Evangelical Lutheran Church in America concludes that "stewardship contacts increase giving." His research claims, "The effect of experience with stewardship contacts appears to be cumulative. The higher the number of contacts reported, the higher the giving level." [Unpublished paper by Edward Uthe, 8765 West Higgins Road, Chicago, IL 60631-4180, page 5, *Asking for Contributions Gets Results,* August 28, 1989.]

Letters have cumulative value. However, the value depends upon both the form and the content of the letters. The best letters for you to send are not the ones written by professionals. "Home-grown writers" communicate more effectively than the distant pro.

This resource includes examples of monthly letters. They should not be copied and mailed. *They are illustrative only!* Their purpose is to start the juices flowing in the writer's imagination. They are not a substitute for creativity.

We started out by asking, "What good is a letter?" That implies a goal for the letter. Before you develop a LETTERS FOR ALL SEASONS program in your church, decide what you want to accomplish. What is the reason for doing the program? What will be the criteria for deciding if it succeeds?

You may define specific financial goals. For example, a church might decide that the goal of the LETTERS program is a defined percentage increase in giving over the comparable period of time from the year before. However, financial goals need not be primary!

You may consider a goal for greater involvement by the people of your congregation. The more people know, the more they will be involved. You can set a goal for a higher percentage of persons who will give both time and money. Make your goals specific. Make them measurable. Make them reasonable. But make yourselves stretch to achieve them.

Some intangible goals are helpful also. Personally, I want people to feel more involved in ministry. I hope that those who give will feel better about their giving. I hope that church leaders will become more assured that they have a story to tell.

The goal for a LETTERS FOR ALL SEASONS program in our church is _____.

CHAPTER II - HOW DO WE DO IT?

In most churches, the Committee on Finance is the group which will take responsibility for the LETTERS FOR ALL SEASONS program. Your church may be the exception to the general rule. Decision-makers in each church must make that decision.

Sometimes the Committee on Finance is made up entirely of "number crunchers" who are excellent with statistics but may not have the gifts for steering a program of this kind. Don't try to force the issue. Two or three enthusiastic persons can carry the project through to a successful conclusion.

In some churches the Work Area on Stewardship will assume this responsibility as their major project. After all, it has more to do with communicating about giving than it does with fund-raising. Even if it is a Stewardship Work Area project, clear lines of communication with the Committee on Finance are essential!

Don't try to work through all of the details with a large committee. Three people are sufficient to put together the proposal (planning) and to guide it to completion (doing).

Do your homework before taking the plan to the Administrative Council or Board. Know what the costs will be. (See page 15 for a guide to estimating costs.) Can the costs be covered by the budget? Is there someone in your congregation who may want to underwrite the extra costs as a special contribution?

LETTERS FOR ALL SEASONS calls for 12 letters, one for each month of the year. Once a month is more effective than a massive barrage over a short period of time. Consistently feeding information in small servings that can be digested is more effective than offering one huge helping of facts. It also spreads out the work load.

Who is going to do the work? When will it get done? Cover only what is necessary in the presentation to the governing group. Anticipate questions which may arise. Answer each question with assurance. If you do not know the answer, promise to get it—then follow through.

Above all else, describe the potential benefits. Describe your dream of what you believe can happen because of this program. Emphasize the goals instead of the mechanical steps. Present the proposal with enthusiasm.

Finally, the proposal is ready. You have chosen your presenter. Next, sit down individually with a few key leaders to discuss your project. What is not clear to them? What questions do they ask? The issues they raise will help you anticipate concerns from the larger group at the Administrative Council or Board meeting.

Ask for approval for a 12-month "experiment." You need a time period long enough to test the value of the program. The members of the board need to know that the experiment has a clearly defined time for evaluation. Your stated goals will be the basis for the evaluation. The request for approvals is not "in perpetuity." After 12 months, if you have not met the goals (if you cannot see any difference) the experiment does not deserve to be continued.

Ask for initial approval *at least* three months prior to beginning the LETTERS FOR ALL SEASONS project. For example, if you start in January, get approval in September. If you start in May, get approval in February.

PLANNING GUIDE

Coordinating group for this program _____

Committee to develop the program for our church:

    1._____
    2._____
    3._____

Benefits of this program for our congregation:

    A)_____
    B)_____
    C)_____

Costs:

    Paper (Letterhead/Stationery) $
    Envelopes $
    Postage $
    Offering Envelopes $
    Brochures, inserts, etc. $
    Other $

Our plan for covering the cost of the program is:

_____

_____

Recommended starting date:

_____

Recommended trial period: 12 months
Presentation to the policy-making unit at our church:

    Date of presentation: _____
    Presenter: _____

Before the presentation, we should discuss it with the following persons:

    1._____
    2._____
    3._____

Note: You may duplicate this planning guide.

CHAPTER III - THE MECHANICS—
WHAT TO DO

For the greatest impact, mail one letter each month. Each letter is to be written by a different person. The monthly letters are not like a "fall financial campaign." Instead, they help provide foundations for the Christian's stewardship of life. They also encourage giving.

Each letter should be written by local people. Models are provided on pages 26-37 to stimulate imagination, not eliminate effort. Encourage creativity by each letter writer.

Remind your writers that the letters will go to *everyone* on your mailing list. They provide an opportunity for witness to inactive members and constituents as well as provide helpful communication to those who are actively involved.

Before any letters are written, decide what will be included in the envelopes with the letters. Including several items in an envelope communicates to people that you are sharing information rather than sending a bill. Stuffing several items in one envelope is a little more work but it is worth it.

We recommend that 5 offering envelopes (6 in months with 5 Sundays) be sent with each mailing. Send one offering envelope for each Sunday plus a special envelope for "gratitude" or special purpose giving.

More than one person regularly give in some families. Where two adult members in one household individually contribute, simply add an extra set of envelopes.

In families where children regularly contribute, send a separate letter to the children. They love to get mail addressed directly to them. It is helpful affirmation for their giving.

If you distribute boxes of envelopes to each giving unit at the beginning of the year, we suggest that you still include a special giving opportunity envelope with each monthly letter.

Time your mailings on several factors. What will work best for the work load of volunteers and office staff? When can materials be gathered (such as quarterly reports)? When are the best times for people to receive the letters?

We suggest that the letters be mailed during the third week of the month. If you are going to include a year-end giving record in the January mailing, the financial secretary will need at least two weeks to prepare the records.

During most months we suggest enclosing a special giving envelope. Experience shows that these envelopes are most effective when received near the end of the month.

When calculating the work load, there is usually no "best time." However, there may be some "worst times." If your church sends out a monthly newsletter, you don't want to deal with it during the same week as your LETTERS FOR ALL SEASONS mailing.

Be consistent. Send the mailing at approximately the same time each month. Develop a routine and stick to it.

Churches that use this system often discover the biggest financial difference in the summer months. When people receive their offering envelopes monthly, they tend to write a check and pay monthly. Churches that use this program will probably experience less negative impact from the summer doldrums.

The following is a suggested monthly outline for an effective series of letters related to each season.

MONTHLY OUTLINE

January

WRITER: Pastor
TOPIC: This is the season of new beginnings. Share the vision of a new year in ministry.
COPY DUE: December 15
MAIL: January 16-23
INCLUDE: A year-end giving record with a "thank you"
A special giving opportunity envelope
A brochure (an attractive promotional brochure for your church)

February

WRITER: Young adult woman from the congregation
TOPIC: A personal testimony can describe the gift in the offering plate as an expression of love for others. Add the suggestion that persons tithe their tax rebate.
COPY DUE: January 15
MAIL: February 16-23
INCLUDE: A brochure about a denominational mission
A special giving opportunity envelope
A schedule of Lenten activities

March

WRITER: A member of the Committee on Finance
TOPIC: Lent and Easter are the themes. Our giving is related to the gift of God expressed in the cross. Our hope in giving is expressed in the Easter story.
COPY DUE: February 15
MAIL: March 16-23
INCLUDE: A special giving opportunity envelope
An announcement of Holy Week services

April

WRITER: A proportionate giver
TOPIC: The decision to give can be according to the amount of resources received. (April 15 is a time when most of us learn about our income.)
COPY DUE: March 15
MAIL: April 16-23
INCLUDE: A letter expressing thanks for giving during the first quarter with a report on ministries of the church
A brochure on tithing
A special giving opportunity envelope

May

WRITER: An older person
TOPIC: The church as family and the mission of the church are important to strengthening family life. Include a paragraph urging persons to write a will as an act of family love. Suggest that they tithe their estate.
COPY DUE: April 15
MAIL: May 16-23
INCLUDE: A brochure: "Including the Church in Your Will"
A return card requesting more information about wills
An announcement of special summer activities (such as Vacation Bible School)
A special giving opportunity envelope

June

WRITER: A schoolteacher or social worker
TOPIC: The pace of life changes as we go into the summer. Urge persons to keep giving regularly during the summer as a spiritual discipline.
COPY DUE: May 15
MAIL: June 16-23
INCLUDE: A special summer giving opportunity envelope
A brochure

July

WRITER: Someone in your church who has been on a work pro-
             ject as a volunteer in mission or someone who serves
             on the board of a church-related home.
TOPIC: Describe what church funds mean to the lives of per-
             sons. Make the letter very personal. Keep statistics to a
             minimum.
COPY DUE: June 15
MAIL: July 16-23
INCLUDE: A letter from the financial secretary expressing thanks
             for giving during the second quarter
             A special offering envelope for a mission project

August

WRITER: A youth who is looking forward to going to college
TOPIC: Express the excitement of the new school year and
             share what the church means to him or her as the time
             comes for living away from home.
COPY DUE: July 15
MAIL: August 16-23
INCLUDE: An announcement of fall start-up activities
             A special giving opportunity envelope for a specific min-
             istry (such as a denominational or local church schol-
             arship fund)

September

WRITER: September is a time when many things start up again in
             most churches. If you are beginning an exciting new min-
             istry this year, have someone write about it with energy!
TOPIC: Let people know that their giving makes such ministry
             possible.
COPY DUE: August 15
MAIL: September 16-23
INCLUDE: A "catch-up" envelope
             A brochure: "Giving Is an Act of Faith"

October

WRITER: A Sunday school teacher with young children or some-
             one who works with a young group can be recruited to
             write this letter.

TOPIC: Tell of the church's ministry to children (or youth) and
            their families through the church.
COPY DUE: September 15
MAIL: October 16-23
INCLUDE: A special giving opportunity envelope for a specific min-
            istry
            A letter expressing thanks for giving during the third
            quarter

November

WRITER: A farmer or gardener
TOPIC: Describe the harvest tradition and the ways of express-
            ing thanks for God's many blessings. Relate the morn-
            ing offering in the worship service to this tradition that
            goes back to Old Testament times.
COPY DUE: October 15
MAIL: November 16-23
INCLUDE: A Thanksgiving offering envelope
            A wills brochure

December

WRITER: Someone who gives very generously. This is probably
            one of the largest givers in the congregation.
TOPIC: The end of the year provides an opportunity for persons
            to "settle up" accounts before the new year begins. It is
            time to take stock of how we have done during the
            year. You can also relate giving to the coming of the
            Magi.
COPY DUE: November 15
MAIL: December 16-23
INCLUDE: A brochure: "Year-End Giving"
            A "Year-End Giving" Envelope

CHAPTER IV - VARIATIONS ON A THEME

Memorial Sunday or All Saints Day

Near the end of May or on the Sunday closest to All Saints Day, you may choose to follow a theme for memorial recognition. A person could write a letter expressing the meaning of lasting memorials. Memorials may honor those who are living or remember those who have died.

+Include a brochure on memorial giving.

+Include an envelope to receive memorial gifts.

If you opt for memorial recognition in May, move the wills emphasis to February or March.

Other Options

Because of special gifts among your people, special ministries of your church, or unique events in the community, the world, or your congregation, you may want to make a major substitution in a particular month. Some possibilities include:

1. A retired pastor expresses thanks for the denominational retirement fund.

2. Missionaries supported by your church or your district tell about their specific ministry.

3. A college student from your congregation who receives a denominationally provided student loan or scholarship can tell what that means to him or her.

CHAPTER V - RECRUITING AND TRAINING WRITERS

Contact each potential writer at least 30 days before the copy is due. If at all possible, make the initial request face to face. Briefly explain the project. Tell the person why you want him or her to write the letter. You affirm the person by extending the invitation.

Tell the potential letter writer that a letter will arrive clearly describing the assignment. Deadlines and writing suggestions will be included. A sample letter will be included, but it is simply an idea starter if inspiration seems slow to come.

Send a letter to your writer the next day after the initial contact. The letter will include:

#Your adaptation of the following recruitment letter.

#A copy of the "General Rules about Writing" (page 24).

#A copy of the sample letter for the month.

#Copies of inserts which will be included with the letter.

Sample "recruitment letter" sent to each prospective letter writer:

Dear _____,

Thank you for agreeing to write a letter during our year-long effort to better communicate with all the people of our congregation. Each letter writer has been specially selected in order to give a wide range of perspectives.

Yours will be one of 12 letters which we send to the entire congregation this year. Your letter will be mailed in the month of _____.

Please focus your letter on _____

_____

Your letter will go in an envelope along with the following items:

_____

_____

_____ *

Turn in your letter to __(person or location)__ no later than __(date)__. If you want the right to approve the edited version before it is sent out, please note that on your copy.

If you have any questions, please ask them. Note the "General Rules" for letter writing we have included.

Grace and Peace,

(signed)
*Include samples of inserts if they are available.

These general rules may be given to each letter writer along with the model for the month that their letter will be mailed:

General Rules about Writing

1. Write conversationally. Visualize telling your story to two or three specific persons in the church.
2. Keep your sentences short. Make sure there are more periods than "ands."
3. Sincerity is more important than cleverness. Write from the heart. You are communicating with people rather than impressing a prize committee on great literature.
4. Relate your story to your own spiritual growth and discipline.
5. Encourage. Be enthusiastic. Don't chastise. Motivate with confidence and hope rather than guilt.
6. The length of the letter is not a major issue. The important matter is clarity and readability.
7. Include a "P.S." if possible. The P.S. is more likely to be read than the body of the letter.
8. We may have to do some editing. Let us know if you want to give final approval before your letter is mailed.

CHAPTER VI - SAMPLE LETTERS

On the following pages you will find sample letters to illustrate the kind of letter recommended for each month. THESE LETTERS SHOULD NOT BE COPIED AND MAILED! This instruction is not because of copyright laws. The letters simply will not apply to every church.

Our purpose in including these letters is to help the LETTERS FOR ALL SEASONS committee and writers understand more clearly the *kind* of letter being suggested.

In some cases, the committee may feel that it is better NOT to provide the sample letter to the writer unless he or she requests a model.

A letter from the pastor looking forward to the church's ministry over the next two years

Dear friends,

Just before the big game an athlete is likely to have a few butter-flies in the stomach. I am writing this letter in December with the recognition that the 199— "game" will have already begun when you read it. Right now, I have butterflies of excitement!

I want to tell you about some of my dreams. I also want to hear about yours. Let's tell one another about those dreams and build a great future for our church as those dreams are powered by God's love.

Prayer has been an area of growth for many persons in our church during the past year. I sense a growing hunger in others to discover a more fulfilling prayer life. I have a dream of several new prayer groups in our life together.

Young adults have been participating in greater numbers recent-ly. I have a dream of several ways our church can help these per-sons cope with the pressures and stress of life. Our church can pro-vide support, encouragement, and training from a Christian perspective on parenting and life choices, as well as Bible instruc-tion and the search for meaning in life.

Worship is the core of our church life together. I have a dream that it can be more helpful to persons who gather each week. The worship committee and I will work to weave the prayers, music, scripture, and sermon into a unity that is richer and more helpful to you and your neighbors.

Last year we took significant steps to meet needs in our commu-nity without stepping back from our relationship to Christian broth-ers and sisters in other parts of the world. I have a dream of more of our members directly relating to the homeless and prisoners in our county.

We can all commit our dreams to God. We can work to see those dreams become reality. We can make a difference. Time and money are needed. They are expressions of what is important.

I invite you to dream, to give, and to work that God's love may be experienced more fully in our lives, in our church, and in our community.

In Christian love,

(signed)

P.S.: Please write down your dreams and visions for our church's ministry and send your list to me.

Model #2

A young adult woman from the congregation

Dear friends,

Have you ever had an experience of new meaning coming from something that you have done hundreds of times? It happened for me last Sunday.

In our worship service, the offering plate was passed down the row where I was sitting. I placed my envelope in the plate. My daughter has her own envelopes. She placed her offering in the plate, too, and we passed it along.

I began thinking about what would happen because of that check in my envelope and the coin in my daughter's envelope. The first image to cross my mind was of my grandmother. She was sick for several months prior to her death. Once every month or two the pastor brought communion to her. Some of the offering paid for the pastor's mileage and salary.

Then I thought of the first pastor I knew. "Doc" was very special to me. He seemed to notice children and took the time to speak to me. Some of that money in the offering plate goes to provide a decent retirement income for retired clergy families.

My TV screen came to mind next. I had just watched a special program on hunger in Africa. Our church sends agricultural workers and engineers to Africa to help people become self-sufficient. We also send preaching missionaries to proclaim the gospel. Some of the check and the coin will reach the other side of the world.

Have you ever thought of the offering as a thrilling time? I never did either—until last Sunday. The thrill comes in remembering the many things that happen because of a check and a coin.

I hope you get a thrill as you place your check, your bill, or your coin in the offering plate the next time it is passed by you in church.

Grace,

(signed)

P.S.: By the way, if you get a tax rebate, why not give 10 percent of it. That tithe of rebates can touch a lot of people for the gospel. It would extend our mission as a congregation!

A member of the Committee on Finance

Dear friends,

The Lenten season is a special time in our church. The hymns have special meaning. The themes that lead up to Easter remind me of the most important beliefs of our faith.

Several years ago I dropped out of college for a year to work for The United Methodist Church. Another dropout and I spent the year helping revitalize youth ministries in churches. We would spend twelve days in a church, then have two days off before going to the next church. It was a great experience.

Families gave us board and room. In fact, almost every meal except breakfast was eaten in a different home. The food was great, but I was often bothered by the kindness of the people. I felt that I had not EARNED their kindness.

Then one day the whole idea of the Lenten and Easter message dawned. None of us deserves (has earned) what God did for us in Jesus Christ. It was a gift. We are asked to honor the giver by accepting the gift we did not merit.

I never have earned God's love, but I can respond to it. That is what we do in the community every time we perform an act of kindness in the name of Christ. That is what we do in church when we give our time and our money.

The Lenten and Easter seasons are traditionally times when giving is at a high level in our church. I think I understand why. When you make your Lenten and Easter offerings this year, I hope you will do so in thankfulness for the gift God has given us in Jesus.

Grace,

(signed)

A person who has found the joy of proportionate giving

Dear friends,

Tax day is almost upon us. I am one of those who usually waits until April 15 to file. Some of us pay our taxes without a whimper. Others of us gripe a lot. I doubt that any of us celebrate the joy of paying taxes.

However, I have been thinking about taxes as they relate to our faith. Jesus and Mary went to Bethlehem to be counted for taxation purposes. Jesus was asked if his followers should pay taxes.

In the Old Testament, the tithe seemed to be a 10 percent tax on crops and livestock. It covered the cost of the priesthood as well as the "Social Security" of that day.

When I file my taxes, it is the one time a year that I am fully aware of our family income. There it is, in black and white. At that time I recognize the proportion of our total income that we give to help others.

This year we decided to raise our giving by 1 percent of our income. That decision has started us on a road we have long wanted to travel. I would like to challenge *you* to match us. Most families can raise their giving at least 1 percent of their income and feel good about it.

Peace,

(signed)

Model #5

A person who has been a member of the congregation for many years

Dear friends,

Fifty-seven years ago, I joined our church. Forty-eight years ago, my husband and I were married at the altar of the church. During those years our church has seen some wonderful times. We have also had a few hard times.

The church has come to mean a lot to me. You feel like family. Most of my close friends are members of this congregation. Can you think of a better place to find friends?

When our children were growing up, we decided we needed to write a will. We didn't have much money, but we had three children who meant more to us than money could calculate. Friends of ours in this congregation agreed to be named in that will to take care of our children if both of us died.

As you may know, the children are now on their own. We have changed our will several times as circumstances have changed. Recently we altered the will so that the church would receive 10 percent of our estate. We are happy to have made that decision.

Forty-eight years ago when we married, we started tithing. Now we know that the practice we began a long time ago will continue to touch the lives of people in Christ's name long after we are gone.

In Christian love,

(signed)

Enc.

P.S.: I have looked over the brochure that is enclosed. Please read it. I hope you will send the return card. Write a will if you don't already have one and include the church in your will.

Model #6

A schoolteacher

Dear friends,

Ah, summer! Most of you know that I am a schoolteacher. For the next three months I will not be sitting up at night grading papers, recording grades, developing tests, and all of those things I usually do after coming home from a day of teaching.

When June comes, I teeter on the edge of burnout. During the school year, each Friday is a "little burnout." I need worship on Sunday. It reminds me of the inner power God gives. It reminds me that all of us face struggles and discouragements in our lives. We all need worship, don't we?

This summer a friend and I plan to take a vacation together. On Sunday mornings we will stop for church wherever we happen to be. Most of these experiences will be really great. During the services I will pray for those of you who are worshiping here in our church.

Before leaving on vacation, I will write a check for my regular church giving. It is much easier and more joyful to do before I leave than after coming back. (Like me, do you spend more on vacation than you intend to?)

The gift before going is great for the church and great for the giver. In other words, everybody wins. I like that.

May you have a wonderful and blessed summer.

Grace,

(signed)

Model #7

Someone who has visited a mission project

Dear friends,

Can you imagine half the population of a city the size of Indianapolis, Indiana, or Nashville, Tennessee, living in an area less than one square mile? I saw it last year and still have a hard time imagining it.

One slum in Bombay, India, fits that description. We walked between houses that provided a 10-by-15-foot room for a family. The paths were narrow. Eaves almost met about five and one half feet over the path. I had to be careful not to hit my head as we wound our way through the maze to the church.

The church began 19 years ago with a handful of people. Now it has over 2000 members. That day about 50 children were seated in a large circle eating their noon meal. Their hair was jet black. Their eyes were bright. Their smiles were winsome.

In addition to participating in the nutrition program, the children are taught to read. They hear Bible stories and they learn songs. They are being related to Jesus Christ and to the Christian community in that slum.

We went upstairs. Women were working at treadle sewing machines. They were learning a trade so they could earn some money. The church made an arrangement with a bank to loan the women money to buy the machines with no interest.

The church can't do everything that calls for action in that slum. However, it is there doing what it can with the resources it has. I was impressed. Our church is in ministry with those people.

When I place a check in the offering plate, I can't help thinking of those smiling children, the sewing women, and the dedication of the church leaders in Bombay. I can't do everything either. None of us can. But we can all do something.

Thankfully,

(signed)

P.S.: Please offer a prayer for Christians in other parts of the world as you give this Sunday. They are doing important work in our Lord's name.

Model #8

A youth in the latter months of high school

Dear friends,

College looked pretty exciting about a year ago. Now that I am just weeks away from leaving for the campus, it is scary.

Some of you may remember what it is like. Will I get along with my roommate? Will the classes be really hard? What happens if . . .? All of those questions are running through my mind.

I want to thank the people of this church for the support they have given me. I remember the children's department. There were not many of us there, but we sang loud!

Our youth class did some really neat things. I got to go to summer camp twice. The church gave half-cost scholarships. That really helped.

Do you remember the time I was an acolyte and the wick burned out before I got to the candles? Yes, there were embarrassing times too.

The Committee on Finance asked me to write this letter. It seemed like a good opportunity to say "thank you" for all you have done to help me learn about the faith and to know God's love.

The college catalog says that there are several college chaplains who work with students on the campus. We provide part of their support through this church. College kids certainly don't have the money to do it. Well, I will try to work with them so you folks get your money's worth.

Be warned! I do intend to come home on holidays. See ya.

Love,

(signed)

An active, enthusiastic, involved church member

Dear friends,

The pace of life changes in September. Vacations end. School starts. Fall flowers bloom. Church activities go into high gear.

At the last meeting of our Council on Ministries I began thinking about the many opportunities we have for spiritual growth through our church. Of course, the list starts out with worship and Sunday school. They complement one another in my life.

This fall we begin a new Bible study called *Disciple*. Our pastor will be leading it over the next thirty-four weeks. It is for anyone who is really serious about studying the Bible. Daily study is expected, plus a two-hour weekly group session. Many of us have been looking for an opportunity like this.

A group in our church spends an afternoon each week doing fix-up and repair work for people in our community who can't get (or can't afford) anyone to make small repairs. It is part of our ministry.

We have others who visit regularly in the hospital. A prayer group meets every week. Youth programs encourage our teenagers. Choir rehearsals are a kind of Christian education. The list can go on and on.

A lot of time and effort goes on behind the scenes so that these opportunities are available to us and to our neighbors. I am thankful for the efforts of both staff and volunteers.

If you are one of those persons who has not been around much this summer, I hope you will make September a catch-up month for your giving. May you also "catch up" with the spiritual growth options that are available this fall.

See you at church!

In Christian fellowship,

(signed)

An adult worker with youth

Dear friends,

Last Sunday a group of youth from our church sat in a circle on the floor of their meeting room. They talked. They talked about school and faith, about vocations and commitment, about relationships and religion.

Sometimes the voices rose. They argued with one another occasionally. They stayed with an idea until all were heard and understood. These youth were dealing with important matters.

What a privilege it was for me to sit in on that meeting. Growing up in this crazy world is scary for youth. But they are not running away. They are hanging in there and trying to draw upon every resource available for the task.

That is one reason our church is so important. All of us, regardless of our age, need the faith resources that the church provides. Youth need our prayers and our encouragement. They need a pat on the back *and* a prayer from the closet.

A portion of our church giving goes into the youth program each year. It is not a big part but it is an important one. We have plenty of room for improvement but I am glad to be a part of a congregation that values youth. How about you?

Grace,

(signed)

A farmer or gardener

Dear friends,

Leaves have changed their color. Most of them have been mulched or bagged. The garden is about finished for the season, and most of the crops are in. This time of year has special significance.

In Old Testament times, portions of the crop were brought into the sanctuary. Thank offerings were a means to express gratitude to the God who provided everything.

Corn shocks in the corners of the sanctuary and cornucopias on the altar remind me of God's creation that provides us with food and fuel. Those symbols also remind me of the heritage that extends back thousands of years.

Every Sunday, when our tithes and offerings are placed on the altar, the ancient tradition is remembered. We no longer bring a bushel of corn or a chicken to the altar. We bring money. We have moved from a world of bartering to a world of cash exchange. But the idea is still there. It is a way of saying, "Thank you, God."

I come to church for many reasons. One of them is to give thanks to God for all of God's goodness. If you feel you have anything to be thankful for, please join me in church this month and express your thanks to God.

Thankfully,

(signed)

A large giver in the church

Dear friends,

Christmas memories seem to grow through the years. I can remember a Christmas many years ago when I left a bucket of oats by the chimney for Santa to feed his reindeer.

I think back to the childhood excitement of receiving gifts. I can also remember the excitement of watching someone unwrap a gift from me. I desperately wanted the one receiving the present to like my gift.

When recalling that time, I realize that gift *giving* and gift *receiving* are two separate events. They may happen about the same time and in the same place, but they are distinct.

Now that I am older I still like to receive gifts. I like to give gifts, too. The size of the gift seems to have little to do with the joy of giving or receiving. A gift always symbolizes a relationship. A gift connects the giver with the receiver.

Our church provides us with opportunities to connect with people throughout the whole world. The magi came to Jesus and brought him gifts from another country. What we give makes a difference to people in this city and to those who live in Calcutta, Nairobi, Hong Kong, and Rio.

Giving starts with Jesus. In him, God offers a *gift*. We are not a part of a business deal. It is in Jesus that giving and receiving really meet. My giving is out of gratitude for the great gift God gave me. Giving and receiving are separate, but they are connected in Jesus.

I would love to *go* with every gift I give, but that isn't possible. When I send a gift through the mail, I think of the person who will be receiving it and I try to imagine the joy on the receiver's face. It is the same way with giving through the church. I imagine a person who is hungry or ill-clad, or someone who has just heard the story of Jesus. After all, Jesus said, "When you have done it unto one of the least of these, you have done it unto me."

Our gifts "connect" with one another and reach out to people all over the world. It is a wonderful privilege. I appreciate it. I hope you do too.

Grace,

(signed)

CHAPTER VII - DESIGN AND DISTRIBUTION

W*hat* we do is important. *How* we do it affects the perception of what is done. The following guides and observations can help people get the message your letter writers want to communicate. The medium can help or hinder the message. Attention to details is important to your effort.

A. For clean copy, print the letters on a laser printer or offset press.

B. Consider a special logo for the year's series of letters.

C. Envelopes with first-class postage are more likely to be read than those with third-class postage. Third-class nonprofit permit mailings require a minimum of 200, and all envelopes must contain *exactly* the same things. No personalized information (such as the report of giving for the previous quarter) may go via third-class postage.

D. The appearance of the envelope will either invite or discourage the receiver. If it isn't opened, it will not be read. You can increase readership by:
   1) hand addressing the envelopes,
   2) using commemorative stamps, and
   3) using envelopes with catchy and colorful logos.

E. The layout of the letter affects readability. Longer letters with wider margins have been found to invite people to read.

SECTION TWO

A
FINANCIAL COMMITMENT
LETTER CAMPAIGN

CHAPTER VIII - A DESCRIPTION

Letters can be an effective means to seek commitments for the ministry and mission budget of your congregation. This chapter will help you determine if this is the right time in your church to have such a campaign.

Most congregations can benefit from the *Letters for All Seasons* monthly letters. Some churches choose to use letters as the primary means of communicating to the members and friends of the congregation when seeking annual financial commitments.

You can have a giving campaign in either the fall or the spring of the year with no visitation, no phone calling, no packets to circulate, and minimal organization. There is still a lot of work. If the time is right, the ratio of response for effort exerted can be very high.

The purpose of a letter-writing financial campaign is different from LETTERS FOR ALL SEASONS. Monthly letters are primarily intended to communicate news of giving and encouragement of giving on a regular basis. The Letter Campaign is *specifically* to seek financial commitments toward the mission and ministry of the local congregation.

A Letter Campaign has certain advantages. It is low key, fairly easy to manage, and makes efficient use of effort. Because of its non-confrontive style, those who react strongly against more rigorous campaigns will find appeal in this method.

Some churches cannot effectively have a visitation program because of the housing arrangements of the membership. If a large number of your members live in condominiums or apartment complexes behind a security guard, you need to find another method of telling the story. Letters may be the best instrument for calling your people to examine their financial commitments through the church.

With letters, you are assured that everyone is getting the same story. In other words, you control the information that is getting through.

A letter-writing campaign requires less organization, fewer workers, and less time than any other kind of campaign. It still must be done with the highest quality. In any organization, priorities must be selected. If many very important things are happening in your church that would be disrupted by a more involved campaign, letters may be the answer this year.

No financial commitment program should be used more than two consecutive years. We recommend that a cycle of methods be used. By setting up the cycle at the beginning of a five-year period, you don't have to struggle with the decision each year.

One cycle may be:

Year 1	Every Member Visitation (using *Celebrate and Visit*, Discipleship Resources, Box 189, Nashville, TN 37202.)
Year 2	*Letters for All Seasons*
Year 3	Group Meetings (Using *Celebrate Together*, available from Discipleship Resources)
Year 4	Commitment Sunday (using *Celebrate Giving* from Discipleship Resources)

A packet circulation program (such as "Off and Running") may be substituted for one of the above suggestions. Approximately every five to ten years a church should consider having a campaign directed by an outside professional. This is especially true if there is a capital funds need.

The letter campaign may be a wise alternative the year after a successful major drive for capital funds. Your people worked hard. They probably spent countless hours and exerted tremendous effort working with a directed Every Member Visitation. Now they are tired. The Letters will give the workers a breathing spell.

Warning: Not every church should have a letter writing financial campaign! This type of campaign is effective *only* if there is good morale in the congregation. When discontent exists, when people do not "feel right" about their church, do not use this method. Conflict is rarely resolved by letters. In those instances, you need a system that will provide opportunity for interpretation and feedback.

Remember, a letter campaign is low key! Churches that plan a bold leap forward should not use the letter writing campaign. If you need to increase your budget by 15 percent or more, this is probably not the method to use.

Mechanics

Suggestions for design and distribution found on page 38 are generally applicable to the financial campaign. There are major procedural differences to take into consideration for the campaign letters. Please follow all of these recommendations!

1. Modify the letters only as needed to communicate more effectively to your congregation.

2. Send the letters to everyone. Include the inactives, the non-residents, and the active non-members.

3. Determine the best way to take into consideration children and youth in this campaign. Youth, along with leaders of children and youth, may form an advisory committee to intentionally include them in every aspect of the campaign.

4. The pastor and/or the chair of the Finance Committee should sign each letter. Never sign a letter, "The Committee." Letters are from individuals to individuals.

5. Do not include unrelated materials with these letters. You can include tracts and commitment cards, but do not use the letter for any other purposes. It will detract from your intent. This is different from our advice on the monthly letters (see page 18).

6. Do not send the budget with the letter. Budgets focus on fund raising. The letters are aimed at giving. There is a difference!

7. Use other means of communication to give a boost to the mail campaign. The pastor should mention the letters from the pulpit. Posters and banners around the church will create an atmosphere of expectancy and celebration.

8. If possible, mail letters on Saturdays so that they arrive on the lighter mail days at the beginning of the week.

9. Pray for the people.

CHAPTER IX - MODEL LETTERS

Three model letters are found on pages 45-50. We suggest that you adapt them, only as necessary, to fit your particular situation.

These campaign letters are longer than one page. You will note the difference in length between these and the LETTERS FOR ALL SEASONS. The twelve monthly letters were primarily for the purpose of communication. These are intended to generate giving commitments. Experience has shown that **long letters are more effective** fund raising tools than short letters. Don't ramble on to make the letter long, but use all the space you need to communicate your message.

Design and print commitment cards or purchase stock cards from a publisher. Make sure you have them in plenty of time. We recommend distributing them in the worship service on the Sunday when you ask for commitments. *Do not send them with campaign letters.*

In a letter campaign, follow-up is extremely important. You will note three sets of follow-up letters. The first (page 51) goes to all those who make a commitment. The primary purposes of this letter are appreciation and acknowledgment.

The second set (pages 52-53) contains two letters to be sent to those who have not responded *and live within the parish area.* Include a copy of the commitment card with each letter.

The third set (pages 54-55) contains two letters to go to *non-residents* who have not responded. Include a commitment card in each of these letters as well.

Send the letter of appreciation (page 51) to all who respond with a commitment to your second or third letter.

Dear friends,

The man had a big knot in his stomach. An important decision had to be made. It had to be made right then! No alternative looked good. In fact, the options looked *terrible.*

Have you ever felt that way? I have. Difficult decisions come to all of us. We may apply for an exemption, but it is never issued.

Some people claim that all we have to do is turn those hard decisions over to Jesus. Frankly, it doesn't always work for me. I pray, but it often feels like God is saying, "You are on your own in this one." In fact, I am convinced that some decisions create a predicament even for God!

God's assurance is needed most when we are not sure of the "answers." Assurance is a special gift of faith. For many of us, the Fanny Crosby hymn, "Blessed Assurance," is a favorite. I suspect we like it because we all hunger for more assurance in our living.

Assurance may come through worship. It is amazing how many times the prayers, sermons, and hymns feel as if they were written especially for me. The scriptures remind us that we are loved even when we make dumb decisions. That is reassuring!

We also find assurance through people—other members of the congregation—who are dependable. In other words, I am confident that they will love me no matter what. I am sure that they would pray for me if they knew of my need.

Prayer groups and Sunday school classes provide opportunities for me to get to know others at deeper levels. Small group opportunities are important for spiritual growth.

One great thing about our church is that we can support one another across age lines. When I was a child I revered a couple of older folks in the church. It is frightening now to realize that a child may be looking up to me. Yet, each of us has something important to share. Young and old need one another.

Our church provides lots of opportunities for support and encouragement. Every time we do something we see another need. It is rather strange, isn't it? Faithfulness usually brings more insight and responsibility.

Our church has meant a lot to people through the years. It means a lot to me. I like to find a quiet place and remember the times and the experiences that helped me "get through" and grow. Can you remember those times when you gave the church an opportunity to minister to you? Remember the times when the church invited you to minister *through* it to others.

People are important. We need to keep doing what we are doing *with* people and *for* people. We also need to reach out to other folks with the good news that God's love and care can be experienced in our worship and in other ways through the life of this church.

Church work that offers assurance costs money. No one needs to apologize for that. Heat in the winter and air conditioning in the summer allow us to concentrate on God rather than worrying about being uncomfortable in worship. We buy materials for Sunday school classes and support mission work around the world. Retired pastors and their families are supported by our giving. The list goes on and on.

Each of us is asked to make a decision over the next few weeks. It is about *giving*. It isn't as hard a decision as the kind I mentioned in the first part of this letter, but it is important. This decision is not about *money* as much as it is about *relationships*.

Our giving (and how we feel about it) tells a lot about what we think about God. Our giving attitudes reflect our attitudes about others. Our giving connects us to God, the Source of all. Our giving also connects us to God's creatures, especially to the "least of these." That's a *lot* of relationships!

We can't go out and buy a day or a month or a year of assurance, but we can respond to the assurance that God gives us. It is on that basis that I give and give regularly. I need a regular reminder that God will not let me go. "Nothing can separate us from the love of God in Christ Jesus our Lord" (Romans 8). Thanks be to God!

Sincerely,

(signed by the chair of the Committee on Finance)

Dear friends,

Six athletes lined up on a track. Their muscles tensed. A man next to the track slowly raised his arm. Each athlete concentrated intently on the tape straight ahead. The official pulled the trigger on the starting gun. The runners burst from the blocks to head for the tape 100 yards from the starting line.

Runners usually have two goals. One is the tape. They can't win by running fast in just any direction. They have to head for the tape. Second, they have a goal that each race will be their personal best. They constantly strive to do better than the time before.

The New Testament writer Paul wrote about "pressing on toward the goal." Jesus talked a lot about the reign (kingdom) of God. God's reign seemed like the goal of all that he said and did.

Goals may be short term (the 100 yard dash) or long term (a marathon). The goal may be winning or merely competing. The variety of goals is as different as people are different.

Some people don't like to set goals. They are afraid that they may not be able to achieve them. New Year's resolutions are like that for many people. They will not make a resolution for fear of breaking it.

I think a goal is more like a guide than a straitjacket. It is a v_sion, not a life sentence. If I set a goal and discover that no road goes there, an alternative goal may need to be set. That's OK.

There are two goals associated with our giving through the church. One is the church's goal of mission and ministry to the world. Our giving is translated into spiritual food and physical food. It teaches children in our Sunday school and offers education for persons around the world. Giving provides opportunities for healing inner hurts within our congregation as well as providing medical missionaries in Africa, Asia, and Latin America.

The second is a goal for personal spiritual growth. We want to become more generous people. For most of us, that is something we grow into rather than achieve instantly.

What I have been leading up to is this: I want to encourage you to set a giving goal. No one else can set that goal but you. All I can do is suggest a goal for those who have never set a giving goal before. That goal is a tithe (or 10 percent). It has its roots in the scriptures and has a long tradition.

Before you commit to your goal, spend some time in prayer. Ask God for some guidance. What difference does God want to make in your life through the goal? Don't give up until you sense some positive direction.

One of the nice things about goals is the fun of working toward them. The first step is to know your starting place. Begin with the percentage of your income that you now give.

What kind of increase will cause you to stretch without discouraging you? An athlete pushes enough for the muscles to grow but not enough to tear the ligaments. Giving becomes spiritually important in our lives when we discover that God's will becomes a factor in the choices we make.

A marathoner has to "sign up" to enter a race. A commitment is made. We need to make such a commitment. In the service on Sunday, *(date)*, you will receive a commitment card. You can use it to write down your goal for this year. The one-year goal is just a step in the longer journey of growing in giving.

I don't run many races any more, but I have found that discipline in my financial life is as important as a training program for a track athlete. My giving is part of my spiritual discipline.

There is an additional benefit. The money you and I give makes a difference in this world. Through it we feed the hungry, heal the sick, help the lame to walk and the blind to see. Through it the poor hear the good news (Luke 4:18-19).

In a real way, the money I give is an investment in the lives of people in the name of Jesus Christ. That investment may not make me wealthy but it certainly has wonderful rewards.

I hope you see the goal of generous giving as a rewarding kind of investment in the development of your own faith discipline as well as in the lives of others around the world.

Sincerely,

(signed by the lay leader)

Dear friends,

The stone fence was about three feet tall. Three children were walking on the sidewalk next to it. One child jumped to the top and began walking along on the four-to-five-inch-wide top of the fence. Her arms waved up and down to keep balance.

You can guess what the companions did. "Boo!" "You're going to fall!" They tried every way they could to distract the fence walker. If concentration were lost, she would fall from the fence.

Most of us have "walked the fence" at one time or another. We, too, experience distractions that bother us when we try to "stay the course." Many things cause us to lose our balance spiritually. Some of these things are in the world and others are a part of our inner life.

I need all the spiritual help I can get. Our church provides needed assistance. It helps me concentrate. It reminds me of the course I need to be on. While others may try to distract me, the church softly encourages me. "Hang in there." "You are not alone."

I remember a story from the Old Testament book of Nehemiah. The Israelites were re-building the Jerusalem wall. Nehemiah's enemies came to distract him. They tried all kinds of tactics. Finally he said, "I am doing a great work and cannot come down."

Nehemiah's answer was an expression of his commitment. He felt called by God to build the wall. Nothing was going to distract him from that task.

Nehemiah's commitment is inspiring. Most of us must confess that many times we have been distracted from what is important to us. We have let the seemingly urgent get in the way of the important. We want that to change.

Discipline and commitment are two key issues. I am not likely to have the commitment if I don't have the discipline. For instance, a tour through the aisles of a grocery store is very different when I have a list from when I am "just shopping."

A major reason I make a financial commitment to our church is my need for personal discipline. A financial commitment makes me look at all of my spending. I can't fulfill the commitment if I wait until the end of the month to see if I have something left over.

I feel better about writing my *first* check of the month to the church rather than waiting to see if I have enough in my account to write the *last* check in the pay period. I think that is why Paul told the Corinthians, "On the *first* day of every week, each of you is to put aside and save . . . [for the collection]" (1 Corinthians 16:2).

Next Sunday, *(date)*, the worship service is designed to help us start or renew the kinds of disciplines we need to live the abundant life. It will be a commitment Sunday. Each of us will be invited to declare our giving intentions for the next year.

Next Sunday can be a time of NEW BEGINNINGS for you as well as a time of renewed faithfulness for the whole congregation. We will celebrate the faith that has come to us through Jesus Christ. Come and worship!

Sincerely,

(signed by the pastor)

Thank You Letter

[Send this letter to all who have made a commitment during the campaign.]

Dear _____,

Each of us finds various opportunities to express our thankfulness to God. Your financial commitment is an important one to the church and, we trust, it is important to you. We want to acknowledge it and express appreciation for your decision to channel your giving through this congregation. Thank you!

Every commitment says something about where we are in our faith and points in a direction we are going. While your financial commitment is important to the church, it is even more important to your spiritual growth and aspirations.

We are glad to report that the total commitments we have received to this date amount to $_____. It appears that we are about ___ percent ahead of last year at this time. This is a strong indication that the ministry and mission of this church will be strong during the year ahead.

Please continue in prayer for the church. Share your dreams and your energies as you share the funds. Together we are "doing a great task and cannot be turned away" from this wonderful mission in the name of Jesus Christ.

Grace and Peace,

(signed by the chair of the Committee on Finance and the pastor)

[Send this letter to resident members who did not make a commitment at the Commitment Sunday Service. Send the letter as early as possible in the week following the service.]

Dear friend,

In her/his last letter, our pastor wrote about Nehemiah building a wall. Walls can be looked at in two ways. They can be seen as something to keep others away or they can be seen as a way to gather folks together.

Last Sunday, we gathered within the walls of our church and had a great service. We remembered who we are and we remembered the important mission Christ has for us in this world. God has given us a great privilege.

It was a time of thanksgiving. We are glad to report the total commitments received amount to $_____. It appears that we are about ____ percent ahead of last year at this date. This is a good indication that the ministry and mission of this church will be strong during the year ahead.

I want to encourage you to make your commitment, too. A commitment card is enclosed. Please bring it to church this Sunday and place it in the offering plate. If you cannot attend, you may mail it to the church.

If you have any questions that those on the Committee on Finance can answer, please ask. We look forward to hearing from you.

Sincerely,

(signed by the chair of the Committee on Finance)

Second Follow-up Letter to Residents

[Send this letter one week after the first follow-up letter, if there has been no response.]

Dear friend,

I want to tell you about an investment opportunity. It will not promise you any more money. It isn't likely to make people stand in awe of you. *Awards* rarely come to those who make this investment. But it has great *rewards.*

This investment helps bring order into life. It offers satisfaction deep within the spirit of the investor. It feeds hungry people. It brings good news to people who thought there was only bad news. It works for justice and peace.

In other words, we are convinced that this investment is in the most important thing in this world: the gospel of Jesus Christ. We have missed your decision to make such an investment and urge you to do it without delay. We think you will find inner satisfaction and joy from making this investment.

This is a serious letter! Our faith indicates that giving is more important to the giver than it is to the church. Secular testimony says the same thing; Dr. Karl Menninger of the Menninger Clinic in Kansas City once remarked that generosity and mental health go hand in hand.

For the good of the gospel, for your own spiritual good, and for the mission and ministry of the church, please fill out the enclosed commitment card and bring it by the church. Our promise is that you will be glad you made such an investment.

Sincerely,

(signed by the lay leader)

[Send this letter to non-resident members who have not made a commitment. Send the letter as early as possible in the week following the service.]

Dear friend,

In her/his last letter, our pastor wrote about Nehemiah building a wall. Walls can be looked at in two ways. They can be seen as something to keep others away or they can be seen as a way to gather folks together.

Last Sunday, we gathered within the walls of our church and had a great service. We remembered who we are and we remembered the important mission Christ has for us in this world. God has given us a great privilege.

It was a time of thanksgiving. We are glad to report the total commitments received amount to $_____. It appears that we are about _____ percent ahead of last year at this date. This is a good indication that the ministry and mission of this church will be strong during the year ahead.

I want to encourage you as a member of our congregation to make your commitment, too. A commitment card is enclosed. Please mail it to the church. It is an important way our non-resident members can participate in this faith community.

If you have any questions that those on the Committee on Finance can answer, please write or phone. We look forward to hearing from you.

Sincerely,

(signed by the chair of the Committee on Finance)

[Send this letter one week after the first follow-up letter if there has been no response.]

Dear friend,

I want to tell you about an investment opportunity. It will not promise you any more money. It isn't likely to make people stand in awe of you. *Awards* rarely come to those who make this investment. But it has great *rewards.*

This investment helps bring order into life. It offers satisfaction deep within the spirit of the investor. It feeds hungry people. It brings good news to people who thought there was only bad news. It works for justice and peace.

In other words, we are convinced that this investment is in the most important thing in this world: the gospel of Jesus Christ. We have missed your decision to make such an investment and urge you to do it without delay. We think you will find inner satisfaction and joy from making this investment.

This is a serious letter! Our faith indicates that giving is more important to the giver than it is to the church. Secular testimony says the same thing; Dr. Karl Menninger of the Menninger Clinic in Kansas City once remarked that generosity and mental health go hand in hand.

For the good of the gospel, for your own spiritual good, and for the mission and ministry of the church, please fill out the enclosed commitment card and bring it by the church. Our promise is that you will be glad you made such an investment.

Sincerely,

(signed by the lay leader)

Enc. (Return addressed envelope) [You may wish to have it stamped]

APPENDIX

Brochures

Brochures can be as different as day is from night. They can be of a variety of sizes, shapes, colors, and content. Imagination is more important than any other single factor. The biggest temptation to overcome is the desire to put more information in the brochure than anyone will want to read.

If you mail a brochure in an envelope with a letter and other materials, the size of the brochure can greatly affect mailing costs. On the other hand, a well-planned brochure has uses beyond the *Letters for All Seasons* program. Printing extra copies for evangelistic and outreach use can reduce unit costs.

You will find two samples of brochures on pages 57-60. Both are simple bifolds. They represent the simplest and cheapest means of developing a brochure.

One brochure lets pictures do all of the communication except for testimonials on the back panel. The other example uses pictures also, but includes brief paragraphs that tell something about the church's ministry.

Your committee is responsible for the story you tell in the brochure. You can communicate more with stories than with facts. If you *must* include numbers, keep them to a minimum!

Develop your brochure to communicate the story of your church's ministry. Select a *few* ministries of the church that you wish to highlight. Choose pictures that will communicate something about that ministry at a glance. Determine if you need to write a brief paragraph to tie the picture to your purpose in producing the brochure. Above all, remember that feelings are more important to convey than facts. Create excitement!

On the back panel of the brochure, print brief testimonials from four or five persons describing what the church (or giving) means to them. Carefully select the persons who write the short comments from among the most respected giving members of your congregation. List the name of each writer with the paragraph.

If you produce a larger brochure, a cover may be purchased commercially. However, consider having an artistic person in your congregation create one especially for you.

Print the brochure on colored paper. Make sure the ink you use will show up well on the paper. Work with a printer to choose paper and ink that will work well when reproducing photos.

What do you want to communicate to your congregation? Remember, one picture is worth a thousand words.

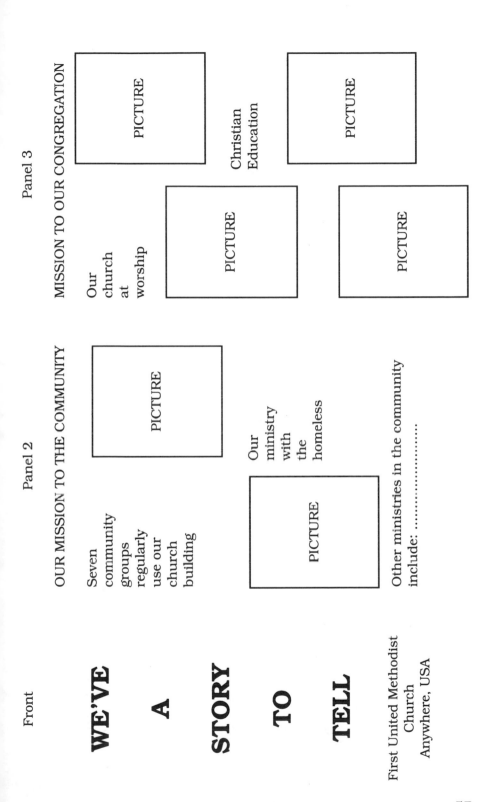

Front

WE'VE
A
STORY
TO
TELL

First United Methodist
Church
Anywhere, USA

Panel 2

OUR MISSION TO THE COMMUNITY

Seven
community
groups
regularly
use our
church
building

PICTURE

Our
ministry
with
the
homeless

PICTURE

Other ministries in the community
include: ....

Panel 3

MISSION TO OUR CONGREGATION

PICTURE

Our
church
at
worship

PICTURE

Christian
Education

PICTURE

PICTURE

MISSION TO THE WORLD

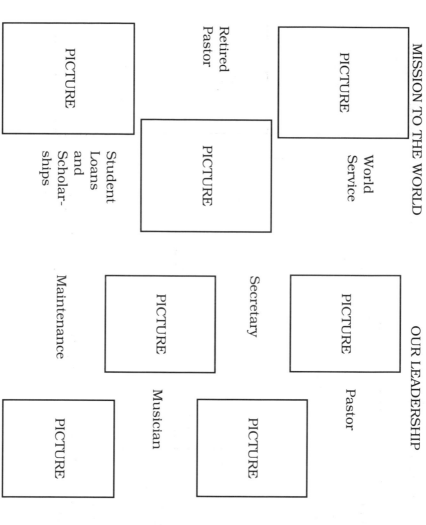

PICTURE — World Service

Retired Pastor

PICTURE

PICTURE

Student Loans and Scholar-ships

OUR LEADERSHIP

PICTURE — Pastor

Secretary

PICTURE

PICTURE

Musician

PICTURE

Maintenance

"When I was 11 years old, I started tithing. Over the years the discipline has helped keep my faith steady. I have never regretted it."

—Ramon Schmidt

"It is easy to lose perspective. Time and money can disappear without any thought. The church helps me to come back to what is ultimately important."

—Linda Blanco

"God has used our church in so many wonderful ways. I am proud that many community groups like Alcoholics Anonymous and English as a Second Language use our rooms. Youth seem to feel at home here.

"As a Christian I want to give. The ministries of our church cause me to rejoice in channeling time and money through this congregation."

—Mary Green

Panel 3

EDUCATION

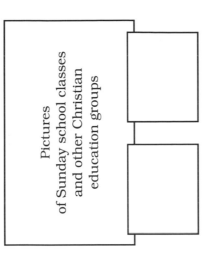

Pictures
of Sunday school classes
and other Christian
education groups

From earliest childhood to the oldest adult, our church provides opportunities for study. We seek to ground all of our study in the biblical faith and to relate learning to life.

Panel 2

OUR OUTREACH

PICTURE
of two
persons
visiting
in a hospital

Maria and Juan are two of our regular team of visitors who call on persons from our church and the whole community who are in the hospital. This is one of many outreach ministries of our church.

PICTURE
of pastor in counseling session
(show back of counselee, face of pastor)

Our pastor counsels with persons within the church and in the community over a variety of family and personal concerns.

Front

A

VITAL

CONGREGATION

OF

FAITHFUL

DISCIPLES

First United Methodist
Church
Anywhere, USA

Panel 4

WORSHIP

When we gather for worship we are reminded of the One who calls us into fellowship and urges us toward growth in faithfulness.

```
PICTURE
of the congregation at wor-
ship
```

Our pastor often takes the Lord's Supper to persons who are home-bound and in nursing homes.

```
PICTURE
of pastor serving commu-
nion to a homebound
person or couple
```

Panel 5

MISSIONS

Our ministry reaches around the world through our participation in the conference and world mission program of our denomination.

```
PICTURE AND DESCRIPTION
of a mission project
within the nation
```

```
PICTURE AND DESCRIPTION
of a mission project
in another land
```

Panel 6

"First Church has brought me into a family with open arms and open hearts. This church is just what I needed."

—Eugenia Jones

"At First Church we have found warm and friendly people who are enthusiastic about faith and life. This church has given us a new beginning."

—Bob and Donna Golding

"First meets me where I am. In my work, my job is to serve the public. It's hard work. First has become a source of peace and strength for me."

—Larry Wallace

"I worked most of my life for a wage. When I retired I felt the need to do something that gave back to this world. The hands-on mission projects of this congregation have opened a new world for me. Thanks, First Church!"

—Tom Wang

SUGGESTED RESOURCES

Church Finance Idea Book by Wayne C. Barrett
An encyclopedia of ideas for commitment campaigns, administration, fund raising, promotion, and planned giving.

Celebrate Giving by Donald Joiner and Herbert Mather
A manual to guide a congregation in planning, developing, and conducting a "commitment Sunday" financial campaign. Includes worship resources, sample letters, and commitment cards.

Celebrate and Visit by Donald Joiner and Juanita Ivie
An "All-Church Visitation" manual. The focus is on ministry instead of money as visits are made to homes to tell the story of the church at work in the world.

Putting God First: The Tithe by Norma Wimberly
A resource for personal study and reflection as well as a guide to group study. Discover tithing as a way of life rather than a numerical duty.

Because God Gives
Selected scripture passages illuminate significant areas of giving.

Becoming a Giving Church by Herbert Mather
Year-round stewardship is rooted in a congregation's sense of worth. Practical ideas will work in churches of all sizes.

Now, Concerning the Offering by Hilbert J. Berger
The why and how of the offering. It can be a meaningful part of every worship service.

Christians and Money by Donald Joiner
Christians struggle with financial goals, setting spending plans, dealing with debt, and planning a will. Here is readable and practical help from a faith foundation.

The Pastor as Steward by Kenneth Carter
> A book to challenge and inform the local church pastor concerning the implication of stewardship in our lives.

Generous People: How to Encourage Vital Stewardship by Eugene Grimm
> Prescription for stewardship including ways we can effectively execute stewardship programs in churches of all sizes.

You Can Run a Capital Campaign: Raising Funds for Special Purposes—A Step-by-Step Guide for Church Leaders
> How to plan a fundraising campaign, recruit and train volunteers, collect pledges, and keep records.

Celebrate Together: A Financial Campaign Using Group Settings by Herb Mather and Don Joiner
> Workbook based on theory that campaigns must change from year to year.

Off and Running
> Sample Packet includes Leader's Guide, postcards, bulletin inserts, estimates of giving card and envelope, poster and runners list. Baton extra.

44 Ways to Expand the Financial Base of Your Congregation
> Practical programs to help you enlarge and solidify the financial structure of your church.